DOVER · THRIFT · EDITIONS

Music

A Book of Quotations

EDITED BY

HERB GALEWITZ

DOVER PUBLICATIONS, INC.
Mineola, New York

DOVER THRIFT EDITIONS

GENERAL EDITOR: PAUL NEGRI
EDITOR OF THIS VOLUME: HERB GALEWITZ

Bibliographical Note

Music: A Book of Quotations is a new work, first published by Dover Publications, Inc., in 2001.

Library of Congress Cataloging-in-Publication Data

Music : a book of quotations / edited by Herb Galewitz.
    p. cm. — (Dover thrift editions)
  ISBN 0-486-41596-1 (pbk.)
    1. Music—Quotations, maxims, etc. I. Galewitz, Herb. II. Series.

PN6084.M8 M86 2001
780—dc21

00-065846

Manufactured in the United States by Courier Corporation
41596105
www.doverpublications.com

Note

Where words fail, music speaks.
HANS CHRISTIAN ANDERSEN

MUSIC is a language all its own, and its charm lies in what it communicates to different people. The same piece of music can open up a wellspring of various emotions, depending on the musician, the listener, and an almost infinite number of other factors. To some, music is a necessary, vital force, affecting one's current mood and state of mind, while to others, it is merely "background noise."

Music has been universally found to have an astounding, positive impact, whether it be physical, emotional, or spiritual. Plato determined that "music is to the mind as air to the body." Oliver Wendell Holmes testified to music's spiritual benefits, advising, "Take a music bath once or twice a week for a few seasons. You will find it is to the soul what a water bath is to the body." As a remedy for any ailment, music has healing powers as well, considered by John A. Logan as "the medicine of the mind," and "the medicine of the breaking heart" to writer Leigh Hunt. Music also offers up refreshment from life's daily grind; as Berthold Auerbach states, "Music washes away from the soul the dust of everyday life."

Quotations from musicians, singers, and composers fill out this collection with witty advice and serious contemplations of music as art. The book encompasses a multitude of musical styles and themes, including classical music, jazz, and opera. Here you'll find biting

criticisms, loving praise, and humorous comparisons. Nearly everyone
has an opinion on the topic of music, and the following is a selection
of over 400 quotations, ranging from the most profound discourse to
some highly facetious remarks. Music as an art has no equal, and its dy-
namic power is as timeless as these memorable observations. The quotations are arranged alphabetically by the author's name.

Music, the greatest good that mortals know,
And all of heaven we have below.

Nothing is capable of being well set to music that is not nonsense.

Music is the only sensual gratification which mankind may indulge in to excess without injury to their moral and religious feelings.

JOSEPH ADDISON

The music teacher came twice each week to bridge the awful gap between Dorothy and Chopin.

GEORGE ADE

When Jack Benny plays the violin, it sounds as if the strings are still back in the cat.

FRED ALLEN

The lady came home from the opera and yet quarreled with her maid.

PETER ALTENBERG

On opera:
Like a husband with a foreign title; expensive to support, hard to understand, and therefore a supreme social challenge.

CLEVELAND AMORY

Definition of a true musician: One who, when he hears a lady singing in the bathtub, he puts his *ear* to the keyhole.

MOREY AMSTERDAM

Where words fail, music speaks.

HANS CHRISTIAN ANDERSEN

Rings on her fingers and bells on her toes,
And so she makes music wherever she goes.

ANONYMOUS (nursery rhyme)

Jazz is not a craze . . . its significance is that it is one of the greatest landmarks of modern art.

GEORGE ANTHIEL

Music exalts each joy, allays each grief,
Expels diseases, softens every pain,
Subdues the rage of poison, and the plague.

JOHN ARMSTRONG

All music is folk music. I ain't never heard a horse sing a song.

When you got to ask what [jazz] is, you'll never get to know.

Every time I close my eyes blowing my trumpet, I look right into the heart of good old New Orleans.

LOUIS ARMSTRONG

No good opera plot can be sensible, for people do not sing when they are feeling sensible.

W. H. AUDEN

Music washes away from the soul the dust of everyday life.

BERTHOLD AUERBACH

The sole end and aim of all music should be nothing else but God's glory and pleasant recreation.

It's easy to play any musical instrument: all you have to do is touch the right key at the right time, and the instrument will play itself.

JOHANN SEBASTIAN BACH

Rugged the breast that music cannot tame.

JOHN CODRINGTON BAMPFYLDE

Competitions are for horses, not artists.

BÉLA BARTÓK

I love Wagner; but the music I prefer is that of a cat hung by its tail outside a window, and trying to stick to the panes of glass with its claws.

CHARLES BAUDELAIRE

Is there a heart that music cannot melt?

JAMES BEATTIE

There are two golden rules for an orchestra . . . start together and finish together. The public doesn't give a damn what goes on in between.

That which penetrates the ear with facility and quits the memory with difficulty.

If an opera cannot be played by an organ-grinder—as Puccini's and Verdi's melodies were played—then that opera is not going to achieve immortality.

I would give the whole of Bach's Brandenburg Concertos for Massenet's Manon and would think I had justly profited by the exchange.

SIR THOMAS BEECHAM

Music is the mediator between the spiritual and the sensual life.

Music should strike fire from the heart of man, and bring tears from the eyes of woman.

LUDWIG VAN BEETHOVEN

Popular music is popular because a lot of people like it.

To me "God Bless America" was not just a song but an expression of my feeling toward the country to which I owe what I have and what I am.

On "There's No Business Like Show Business":
I wrote it as a so-called "throwaway" to cover a stage wait. No one visualized what the song would eventually become, especially myself.

There's no such thing as a new melody. Our work is to con-
nect the old phrases, so that they will sound like a new tune.

IRVING BERLIN

Every composer knows the anguish and despair occasioned
by forgetting ideas which one has no time to write down.

HECTOR BERLIOZ

Music . . . can name the unnamable and communicate the
unknowable.

I'm not interested in having an orchestra sound like itself. I
want it to sound like the composer.

LEONARD BERNSTEIN

When the morning stars sang together, and all the sons of
God shouted for joy.

THE BIBLE (Old Testament; Job)

The Fiddle: An instrument to tickle human ears by friction
of a horse's tail on the entrails of a cat.

AMBROSE BIERCE

Music wasn't made to make us wise, but better natured.

JOSH BILLINGS

How nice the human voice is when it isn't singing.

The opera always loses money. That's as it should be. Opera has no business making money.

RUDOLPH BING

Debussy is like a painter who looks at his canvas to see what more he can take out; Strauss is like a painter who has covered every inch and then takes the paint he has left and throws it at the canvas.

ERNEST BLOCH

On hearing George Gershwin's Porgy *and* Bess:
Oh well, he did not know how to write an opera. There is no continuity, only a series of numbers.

NADIA BOULANGER

Music is our fourth great material want—first food, then raiment, then shelter, then music.

CHRISTIAN NESTELL BOVEE

Chamber music—a conversation between friends.

CATHERINE DRINKER BOWEN

When you see a lovely woman for a long time, a woman who is at once gracious and tender and pure, you cannot help being inspired by the spectacle.

Passion is not natural to mankind; it is always an exception, an excrescence.

JOHANNES BRAHMS

God is its author, and not man; he laid the keynote of all harmonies . . . and he made us so that we could hear and understand.

JOHN G. BRAINARD

Music hath charms to soothe the savage beast.

JAMES BRAMSTON

It is cruel . . . that music should be so beautiful. It has the beauty of loneliness and of pain: of strength and freedom. The beauty of disappointment and never-satisfied love. The cruel beauty of nature, and everlasting beauty of monotony.

The old idea . . . of a composer suddenly having a terrific idea and sitting up all night to write it is nonsense. Nighttime is for sleeping.

BENJAMIN BRITTEN

For there is music wherever there is harmony, order, or proportion.

Sure there is music even in the beauty, and the silent note which Cupid strikes, far sweeter than the sound of an instrument.

For even that vulgar and tavern music, which makes one man merry, another mad; strikes in me a deep fit of devotion, and a profound contemplation of the first Composer; there is something in it of divinity more than the ear discovers.

SIR THOMAS BROWNE

Who hears music feels his solitude peopled at once.

ROBERT BROWNING

Life can't be all bad when for ten dollars you can buy all the Beethoven sonatas and listen to them for ten years.

The Beatles are not merely awful. . . . They are so unbelievably horrible, so appallingly unmusical, so dogmatically insensitive to the magic of the art, that they qualify as crowned heads of antimusic.

WILLIAM F. BUCKLEY, JR.

Music, once admitted to the soul, becomes a sort of spirit, and never dies.

EDWARD GEORGE BULWER-LYTTON

The best music should be played as the best men and women should be dressed—neither so well nor so ill as to attract attention to itself.

To know whether you are enjoying a piece of music or not you must see whether you find yourself looking at the advertisements of Pear's Soap at the end of the libretto.

SAMUEL BUTLER

A thousand hearts beat happily; and when
    Music arose with its voluptuous swell,
Soft eyes look'd love to eyes which spake again,
    And all went merry as a marriage bell
But hush! hark! a deep sound strikes like a rising knell.

There's music in the sighing of a reed;
    There's music in the gushing of a rill;
There's music in all things, if men had ears:
    Their earth is but an echo of the spheres.

LORD BYRON (GEORGE GORDON)

Nobody dreams of music in hell, and nobody conceives of heaven without it.

S. PARKES CADMAN

When we separate music from life we get art.

New music: new listening. Not an attempt to understand something that is being said, for, if something were being said, the sounds would be given the shapes of words. Just an attention to the activity of sounds.

JOHN CAGE

If you can sell green toothpaste in this country, you can sell opera.

SARAH CALDWELL

The blues were the gateway to freedom for all American Negroes.

E. SIMMS CAMPBELL

A lot of people are singing about how screwed up the world is, and I don't think that everybody wants to hear about that all the time.

MARIAH CAREY

Music is a kind of inarticulate, unfathomable speech, which leads us to the edge of the infinite, and impels us for a moment to gaze into that.

See deep enough and you see musically.

All deep things are song. It seems somehow the very central essense of us, song; as if all the rest were but wrappers and hulls.

Music is well said to be the speech of angels; in fact, nothing among the utterances allowed to man is felt to be so divine. It brings us near to the infinite.

THOMAS CARLYLE

My idea of Heaven is to be able to sit and listen to all the music by Victor Herbert that I want to.

ANDREW CARNEGIE

I invariably play some Bach to start the day. But on the piano, not the cello, and usually preludes and fugues. It is like a benediction on the house.

The cello is like a beautiful woman who has not grown older, but younger with time, more slender, more supple, more graceful.

For me, Bach is like Shakespeare. He has known all and felt all. He is everything.

PABLO CASALS

There can be no mischief sure when there is music.

MIGUEL DE CERVANTES

On opera:
A magic scene contrived to please the eyes and ears at the expense of understanding.

In a garden where there are no birds, a croaking toad is a nightingale.

FYODOR CHALIAPIN, *singer*

If you love music, hear it; go to operas, concerts, and pay fiddlers to play to you; but I insist upon your neither piping nor fiddling yourself. It puts a gentleman in a very frivolous contemptible light.

LORD CHESTERFIELD

Music is a prophecy of what life is to be, the rainbow of promise translated out of seeing into hearing.

MRS. CHILD

Military justice is to justice as military music is to music.

GEORGES CLEMENCEAU

Music indeed! Give me a mother singing to her clean and fat and rosy baby.

WILLIAM COBBETT

Dialogue is just lyrics that don't rhyme.

NAT "KING" COLE

The best sort of music is what it should be—sacred; the next best, the military, has fallen to the lot of the devil.

Swans sing before they die—'twere no bad thing
Should certain persons die before they sing.

SAMUEL TAYLOR COLERIDGE

Indeed Musick, when rightly ordered, cannot be prefer'd too much. It composes the Passions, affords a strong Pleasure, and excites a Nobleness of Thought.

JEREMY COLLIER

O Music! sphere-descended maid.
Friend of Pleasure, Wisdom's aid!

WILLIAM COLLINS

Someday we may have as many followers as the harpsichord.

EDDIE CONDON, *jazz musician*

Music alone with sudden charms can bind
The wand'ring sense, and calm the troubled mind.

Music hath charms to soothe a savage breast,
To soften rocks, or bend a knotted oak.

WILLIAM CONGREVE

Without music, life is a journey through a desert.

PAT CONROY

Cocktail music is accepted as audible wallpaper.

ALISTAIR COOKE

Is there an American way of performing Schubert as distinguished from an Austrian way? It seems to me that there most definitely is.

So long as the human spirit thrives on this planet, music in some living form will accompany and sustain it and give it expressive meaning.

Composers tend to assume that everyone loves music. Surprisingly enough, everyone doesn't.

AARON COPLAND

To sing man's melody is only a vain show of art. God cannot take delight in praises where the man of sin has a hand in making the melody.

REV. JOHN COTTON

Extraordinary how potent cheap music is.

NOEL COWARD

How soft the music of those village bells
Falling at intervals upon the ear
In cadence sweet!

WILLIAM COWPER

I think popular music in this country is one of the few things in the 20th century that have made great strides in reverse.

BING CROSBY

If there were a conservatory in Hell, if one of its talented students were instructed to write a program symphony on "The Seven Plagues of Egypt," and if he were to compose a symphony like Mr. Rachmaninoff's, then he would have fulfilled his task brilliantly and would bring delight to the inhabitants of Hell.

CESAR CUI, *reviewer*

It is far better to be the first musician in Elmira than one of
10,000 in New York.

WALTER DAMROSCH

Music was known and understood before words were spoken.

CHARLES DARWIN

> Adding once more the music of the tongue
> To the sweet speech of her alluring eyes.

SIR JOHN DAVIES

I think that one of the greatest dangers that faces people in
this country is the tyrants who would come in and solve your
crimes by putting a rock festival in every park.

EDWARD MICHAEL DAVIS

Had Wagner been a little more human, he would have been
truly divine.

The idea of marketing a musical composition like a tub of
lard or a barrel of beer is to me as sad as it is ridiculous.

On opera:
A form of entertainment where there is always too much
singing.

CLAUDE-ACHILLE DEBUSSY

Sweet popular music is claptrap in the main, and the main is
where it belongs.

The tuba is certainly the most intestinal of instruments, the very lower bowel of music.

PETER DE VRIES

[Igor Stravinsky] is constantly on the move, seeking out at every step how to deny the very thing that he has been in his previous works.

SERGEI DIAGHILEV

Composers shouldn't think too much—it interferes with their plagiarism.

HOWARD DIETZ

It is safe to say that no man ever went wrong, morally or mentally, while listening to a symphony.

JUDGE JOHN J. DILLON

O Music! Miraculous art! A blast of thy trumpet and millions rush forward to die; a peal of thy organ and uncounted nations sink down to pray.

BENJAMIN DISRAELI

There is a spirituality about the face, however . . . which the typewriter does not generate. The lady is a musician.

SIR ARTHUR CONAN DOYLE

Crave the tuneful nightingale to help with her lay,
The ousel and the throstlecock, chief music of our May.

MICHAEL DRAYTON

The trumpets loud clangour
Excites us to arms.

What passion cannot music raise and quell?

So when the last and dreadful hour
This crumbling pageant shall devour,
The trumpet shall be heard on high,
The dead shall live, the living die,
And Music shall untune the sky!

JOHN DRYDEN

Music was invented to confirm human loneliness.

LAWRENCE DURRELL

It's not me. It's the songs. I'm just the postman. I deliver the songs.

He's singing all his own songs. That ain't no folk singer. Folk singers sing those old folk songs, ballads.

BOB DYLAN

This world may consist of musical notes as well as of mathematical rules.

Never did Mozart write for eternity, and it is for precisely that reason that much of what he wrote is for eternity.

ALBERT EINSTEIN

'Tis God gives skill,
But not without men's hands: He could not make

Antonio Stradivari's violins
Without Antonio.

GEORGE ELIOT

You are the music while the music lasts.

T. S. ELIOT

I don't like to look back because it destroys my perspective of writing music.

Playing "bop" is like playing Scrabble with all the vowels missing.

It don't mean a thing if it ain't got that swing.

DUKE ELLINGTON

And music pours on mortals
Her magnificent disdain.

Music is the poor man's Parnassus.

RALPH WALDO EMERSON

Jazz is the expression of protest against law and order, the bolshevik of license striving for expression in music.

ANNE SHAW FAULKNER

Jazz without the beat, most musicians know, is a telephone yanked from the wall; it just can't communicate.

LEONARD FEATHER

Oh, the brave music of a *distant* drum.

EDWARD FITZGERALD

The word jazz in its progress toward respectability has meant first sex, then dancing, then music.

F. SCOTT FITZGERALD

Music comes first from my heart, and then goes upstairs to my head where I check it out.

ROBERTA FLACK

Composing is like making love to the future.

LUKAS FOSS

I'd hate this to get out, but I really like opera.

FORD FRICK, *baseball commissioner*

Bach almost persuades me to be a Christian.

ROGER FRY

Give the piper a penny to play and two pence to leave off.

Music is nothing else but wild sounds civilized into time and tune.

THOMAS FULLER

Nobody really sings in an opera—they just make loud noises.

I make my reputation while the curtain is up, not while it is down.

AMELITA GALLI-CURCI, *singer*

Opera is when a guy gets stabbed in the back and instead of bleeding, he sings.

ED GARDNER

Jazz I regard as an American folk music; not the only one, but a very powerful one which is probably in the blood and feeling of the American people more than any other style of folk music.

Making music is actually little else than a matter of invention aided and abetted by emotion.

True music must repeat the thought and inspirations of the people and the time. My people are Americans and my time is today.

It sounds simple, of course, but personally I can think of no more mentally arduous task than making music.

GEORGE GERSHWIN

Music, in the works of its greatest masters, is more marvellous, more mysterious, than poetry.

H. GILES

Mozart is the human incarnation of the divine force of creation.

Music fills up the present moment more decisively than anything else, whether it awakens thought or summons to action.

Music in the best sense has little need of novelty; on the contrary, the older it is, the more one is accustomed to it, the greater is the effect it produces.

JOHANN VON GOETHE

Popular music . . . is a frankly commercial pursuit. It thus tends to establish formulas, to turn out a product of robots, by robots and for robots.

A history of song, especially popular song, may contain, deeply imbedded, the history of a people.

America has more than one music, and that the authenticity of its various musics lies beneath geographical divisions and racial quotas.

ISAAC GOLDBERG

Women and music should never be dated.

OLIVER GOLDSMITH

BENNY GOODMAN: I'm extremely sorry, Mr. Bartók, but it would be impossible to play what you have written for the clarinet unless I can acquire a third hand.

BÉLA BARTÓK: Very well, then—approximate!

On integrating Negroes into his band:
If a guy's got it, let him give it. I'm selling music, not prejudice.

BENNY GOODMAN

Mr. Presley has no discernable singing ability. His specialty is rhythm songs which he renders in an undistinguished whine; his phrasing, if it can be called that, consists of the stereotyped variations that go with a beginner's aria in a bathtub.

JACK GOULD, *music critic*

I know only two tunes. One of them is "Yankee Doodle"—
and the other isn't.

ULYSSES S. GRANT

A jazz musician is a juggler who uses harmonies instead of
oranges.

BENNY GREEN

The best way to get to knowing any bunch of people is to go
and listen to their music.

WOODY GUTHRIE

On composer Richard Rodgers:
I hand him a lyric and get out of his way.

OSCAR HAMMERSTEIN II

To my way of thinking, Bessie Smith was the greatest artist
American jazz ever produced; in fact, I am not sure that her art
did not reach far beyond the limits of the term "jazz."

The hysterical roars of the crowd which once had been sweet
music to Benny Goodman's ears, first perplexed, then irked
him. He wanted his music to be appreciated for its essential
worth and not because of its fortissimo volume and crazy antics.

JOHN HAMMOND

Wagner's star will continue to shine in the German operatic
firmament—as long as all around is darkness.

Wagner's operatic style recognizes only superlatives, and a superlative has no future. It is the end, not the beginning.

EDUARD HANSLICK

Emotion, not thought, is the sphere of music.

REV. HUGH REGINALD HAWEIS

I occasionally play works by contemporary composers and for two reasons. First to discourage the composer from writing any more and secondly to remind myself how much I appreciate Beethoven.

If I don't practice one day, I know it: two days, the critics know it: three days, the public knows it.

The new technique of recording makes it possible to get all sorts of new sounds. But some of them were not meant for human ears. They were meant for hounds . . . I am old fashioned enough to believe that the musical side of the performance is what counts.

When people come to play music as they do to play bridge, civilization will have taken the longest stride forward since the beginning of time.

JASCHA HEIFETZ

Out of my own great woe,
I make my little songs.

When words leave off, music begins.

HEINRICH HEINE

Music helps not the toothache.

GEORGE HERBERT

Song—The licensed medium for bawling in public things too silly or sacred to be uttered in ordinary speech.

Perhaps it was because Nero played the fiddle, they burned Rome.

OLIVER HERFORD

Why should the devil have all the good tunes?

ROWLAND HILL

There's only one woman I know of who could never be a symphony conductor, and that's the Venus de Milo.

MARGARET HILLIS, *director of the Chicago Symphony*

Music is a strange bird singing the songs of another shore.

J. G. HOLLAND

Without Elvis, none of us could have made it.

BUDDY HOLLY

Alas for those that never sing,
But die with all their music in them!

Take a music bath once or twice a week for a few seasons. You will find it is to the soul what a water bath is to the body.

Those who have no ear for music must be very careful how they speak about that mysterious world of thrilling vibrations which are idle noises to them.

OLIVER WENDELL HOLMES

For bells are Music's laughter.

THOMAS HOOD

> Elected Silence, sing to me
> And beat upon my whorled ear,
> Pipe me to pastures still and be
> The music that I care to hear.

GERARD MANLEY HOPKINS

Her singing was mutiny on the high C's.

HEDDA HOPPER

Music is an incitement to love.

There is a fault common to all singers. When they're among friends and are asked to sing they don't want to, and when they're not asked to sing they never stop.

HORACE

False notes (at a piano concert) are human. Why does everything have to be perfect? You know, perfection itself is imperfection.

I am a general. My soldiers are the keys, and I have to command them.

VLADIMIR HOROWITZ

As we grow older we find our admiration increasing for the girl who can't play without the music she has left at home.

ED HOWE

Music is making manifest to our dull ears the divine harmony of the universe, and through music, we read the universal.

The only one of the arts that can be prostituted to a base use.

An attempt to describe emotions that are beyond speech.

ELBERT HUBBARD

Music expresses that which cannot be said and on which it is impossible to be silent.

VICTOR HUGO

Miss Truman is a unique American phenomenon with a pleasant voice of little size and fair quality. . . . There are few moments during her recital when one can relax and feel confident that she will make her goal, which is the end of the song.

PAUL HUME, *music critic*

The only art . . . wherein originality may reveal itself in the face of fools and not pierce their mental opacity.

JAMES G. HUNEKER

Music is the medicine of the breaking heart.

LEIGH HUNT

After silence, that which comes nearest to expressing the inexpressible is music.

ALDOUS HUXLEY

[Leonard] Bernstein could no doubt write fugues around Irving Berlin with great skill and ease, but he has as yet to write as beautiful and as inspired a song as "I Got Lost in His Arms" [from *Annie Get Your Gun*].

EDWARD JABLONSKI

Blues are the songs of despair, but gospel songs are the songs of hope.

MAHALIA JACKSON

Rock 'n' roll music is for adolescents. It's a dead end.

MICK JAGGER

In music the blacks are generally more gifted than the whites, with accurate ears for tune and time; and they have been found capable of imagining a small catch. Whether they will be equal to the composition of a more extensive run of melody, or of complicated harmony, is yet to be proved.

THOMAS JEFFERSON

The history of a people is found in its songs.

GEORGE JELLINEK

When I started, it was all about getting girls. It had nothing to do with money.

BILLY JOEL

It is from the blues that all that may be called American music derives its most distinctive characteristics.

JAMES WELDON JOHNSON

Of all noises I think music is the least disagreeable.

The only sensual pleasure without vice.

Had I learned to fiddle, I should have done nothing else.

The Italian opera [in London], an exotic and irrational
entertainment.

SAMUEL JOHNSON

Let me have music dying, and I seek
No more delight.

Give me books, fruit, French wine and fine weather and a
little music out of doors, played by somebody I don't know.

Heard melodies are sweet, but those unheard
Are sweeter; Therefore, ye soft pipes, play on;
Not to the sensual ear, but, more endear'd,
Pipe to the spirit ditties of no tone.

JOHN KEATS

The conductor has the advantage of not seeing the audience.

ANDRE KOSTELANETZ

I never play now except for my own pleasure, and there's not
much pleasure in playing for yourself.

FRITZ KREISLER

The sweetest music is the sound of the voice of the woman
we love.

JEAN DE LA BRUYÈRE

I even think that sentimentally I am disposed to harmony.
But organically I am incapable of a tune.

CHARLES LAMB

Music is God's best gift to man, the only art of heaven given
to earth, the only art of earth we take to heaven.

WALTER SAVAGE LANDOR

I never practice: I always play.

WANDA LANDOWSKA, *harpsichordist*

Music is love in search of a word.

SIDNEY LANIER

The chromatic scale is what you use to give the effect
of drinking a quinine martini and having an enema
simultaneously.

PHILIP LARKIN

The concert halls and opera houses in the late 19th and
early 20th centuries were filled with groups of people who
made music, as music lovers do for their own pleasure at
home, and who constituted the finest, most critical, and also
most appreciative public.

There are three worlds of music—the composers, the
performers and the critics.

When I hear (alas, so often) somebody stating with great
rectitude that he never changes an iota in the printed score,

I know by that one statement that I am listening to a person ignorant of the relativity in music notation.

ERICH LEINSDORF

I don't know which will go first—rock 'n' roll or Christianity.

We're more popular than Jesus Christ now.

JOHN LENNON

Leonard Bernstein has been describing musical secrets that have been well known for over 400 years.

I think a lot of [Leonard] Bernstein—but not as much as *he* does.

"Tell me, George [Gershwin], if you had to do it all over, would you fall in love with yourself again?"

A symphonic conductor . . . has already made the impression that eventually determines the extent of his success or failure— on the members of the orchestra, whose attitude toward any new conductor may be epitomized as "a hundred men and a louse."

OSCAR LEVANT

Words for music are like water-weed: they only live in the streams and eddies of melody.

DAY LEWIS

You can have either *The Resurrection* or you can have Liberace. But you can't have both.

LIBERACE

Show me an orchestra that likes its conductor and I'll show
you a lousy conductor.

GODDARD LIEBERSON

There's sure no passion in the human soul,
But finds its food in music.

GEORGE LILLO

Music is the medicine of the mind.

JOHN A. LOGAN

Music has a poetry of its own, and that poetry is called
melody.

Music itself is the purest expression of emotion. To me,
emotion is the guts of the theatre. With music you can say
in one moment what an author would take a whole scene
to tell you in a drama.

JOSHUA LOGAN, *theatrical producer*

When she had passed, it seemed like the ceasing of exquisite
music.

Yea, music is the Prophet's art
Among the gifts that God hath sent,
One of the most magnificent!

And the night shall be filled with music,
And the cares, that infest the day,
Shall fold their tents, like the Arabs,
And as silently steal away.

Show me the home wherein music dwells, and I shall show you a happy, peaceful, and contented home.

> He is dead, the sweet musician!
> He has gone from us forever,
> He has moved a little nearer
> To the Master of all music.

Music is the universal language of mankind.

HENRY WADSWORTH LONGFELLOW

We must teach music in schools; a schoolmaster ought to have skill in music or I would not regard him.

(Music) The art of the prophets, the only art that can calm the agitations of the soul; it is one of the most magnificent and delightful presents God has given us'.

Music makes more people milder and gentler, more moral and more reasonable.

I am not satisfied with any man who despises music. For music is a gift of God.

MARTIN LUTHER

People whose sensibility is destroyed by music in trains, airports, lifts, cannot concentrate on a Beethoven Quartet.

WITOLD LUTOSLAWSKI

Music, the mosaic of the Air.

ANDREW MARVELL

Modern music is as dangerous as narcotics.

PIETRO MASCAGNI

A hundred years from now, people will listen to the music of the Beatles the same way we listen to Mozart.

PAUL MCCARTNEY

Regard your voice as capital in the bank. When you go to sing, do not draw on your bank account. Sing on your interest and your voice will last.

LAURITZ MELCHIOR

If the king loves music, there is little wrong in the land.

MENCIUS

The music critic, Huneker, could never quite make up his mind about a new symphony until he had seen the composer's mistress.

Opera in English is, in the main, just about as sensible as baseball in Italian.

H. L. MENCKEN

Through "Amahl" I learned to write an opera for children. At the premieres, I always watch the audience. If a child asks to go to the bathroom, I know I've failed.

GIAN CARLO MENOTTI

The Russian Jewish child of past generations, with his urban, restricted and precarious life, and highly charged emotions, found his sole expression in the playing of his violin with the result that so many violinists from that time onwards come of that same origin.

The violinist is that peculiarly human phenomenon distilled to a rare potency—half tiger, half poet.

To play great music, you must keep your eyes on a distant star.

YEHUDI MENUHIN

I can hold a note as long as the Chase National Bank.

ETHEL MERMAN

If you think you've hit a false note, sing loud. When in doubt, sing loud.

ROBERT MERRILL

There is nothing in the world so much like prayer as music is.

WILLIAM P. MERRILL

The power of music is so great that in the legends of all nations, the invention of the art is ascribed to the gods.

KARL MERZ

Even before the music begins there is that bored look on people's faces. A polite form of self-imposed torture, the concert.

Music is a beautiful opiate, if you don't take it too seriously.

HENRY MILLER

The piano is able to communicate the subtlest universal truths by means of wood, metal and vibrating air.

KENNETH MILLER

Such sweet compulsion doth in music lie.

JOHN MILTON

Let me die to the sounds of delicious music.

Last words of MIRABEAU

I never use a score when conducting my orchestra. . . . Does a lion tamer enter a cage with a book on how to tame a lion?

Only life suffered can transform a symphony from a collection of notes into a message for humanity.

DMITRI MITROPOULOS, *conductor*

Beethoven had real prospects as a composer. If he had lived longer, he might have fulfilled his promise.

PIERRE MONTEUX, *conductor*

Wherever there is good music there is harmony. Wherever there is harmony there are good citizens.

J. HAMPTON MOORE

Sing-sing—Music was given,
To brighten the gay and kindle the loving.

Those evening bells! those evening bells!
How many a tale their music tells,
Of youth, and home, and that sweet time
When last I heard their soothing chime.

THOMAS MOORE

Music, of all the arts, has the greatest influence over
the passions, and the legislator ought to give it the greatest
encouragement.

NAPOLEON

I care not who writes the laws of a country so long as I may
listen to its songs.

GEORGE JEAN NATHAN

The good composer is slowly discovered, the bad composer is
slowly found out.

Is there something in the viola that develops exceptional
intelligence in its executants, or is it just that when a man has
exceptional intelligence he takes up the viola as a matter of
course?

ERNEST NEWMAN

La Sonnambula is dull enough to send the most athletic
sleepwalker back to bed.

NEWSWEEK

Liszt, or the Art of Running After Women.

Without music life would be a mistake.

Is Wagner a human being at all? Is he not rather a disease?

FRIEDRICH WILHELM NIETSCHE

Wagner's music is better than it sounds.

BILL NYE

Music does all our joys refine,
And gives the relish to our wine.

JOHN OLDHAM

Music is another lady that talks charmingly and says nothing.

AUSTIN O'MALLEY

We are the music-makers,
And we are the dreamers of dreams,
Wandering by lone sea-breakers,
And sitting by desolate streams.

A. O'SHAUGHNESSY

Music is your own experience, your own thoughts, your wisdom. If you don't live it, it won't come out of your horn. They teach you there's a boundary line to music. But, man, there's no boundary line to art.

CHARLIE PARKER

In fact, dance rhythm may be securely asserted to have been the immediate origin of all instrumental music.

SIR H. C. PARRY

All art constantly aspires towards the condition of music.

WALTER HORATIO PATER

Music is an invisible dance, as dancing is a silent music.

Music is the only one of the fine arts in which not only man, but all other animals, have a common property.

JEAN PAUL

I tried to resist his overtures, but he plied me with symphonies, quartettes, chamber music, and cantatas.

S. J. PERELMAN

You see, our fingers are circumcised . . . which gives them very good dexterity, particularly in the pinky.

ITZHAK PERLMAN

I would choose [Ferdinand] Hiller for my friend, Chopin for my husband, Liszt for my lover.

POLISH COUNTESS PLATER

Music is to the mind as air to the body.

PLATO

Music resembles poetry; in each
Are nameless graces which no methods teach,
And which a master-hand alone can reach.

Some to church repair,
Not for the doctrine, but the music there.

ALEXANDER POPE

My sole inspiration is a telephone call from a producer.

COLE PORTER

Music rots when it gets too far from the dance.

EZRA POUND

I don't know anything about music. In my line you don't
have to.

ELVIS PRESLEY

I do not know what I was playing,
Or what I was dreaming then;
But I struck one chord of music,
Like the sound of a great Amen.

ADELAIDE ANNE PROCTER

When Scriabin played his Fifth Sonata, every note soared.
With Rachmaninoff all the notes lay on the ground.

SERGEI PROKOFIEV

When that fellow [Toscanini] gets a score into his hands, he
digs into it like a miner in order to explore every corner.

GIACOMO PUCCINI

Musick and poetry have ever been acknowledged Sisters, which walking hand in hand support each other.

HENRY PURCELL

Music is not a science any more than poetry is. It is a sublime instinct, like genius of all kinds.

LOUISE DE LA RAMÉ

If anyone has conducted a Beethoven performance, and then doesn't have to go to an osteopath, then there's something wrong.

SIMON RATTLE

A violinist can hide in the Brahms Concerto, where bad taste and musical inadequacies won't show up as easily as they do in Mozart.

RUGGIERO RICCI

Music is the poetry of the air.

Music is the moonlight in the gloomy night of life.

JEAN PAUL RICHTER

Music is for certain among us, more than a pleasure; it is a necessity.

ROMAIN ROLLAND

If music could be translated into human speech, it would no longer need to exist.

To the social-minded, a definition for Concert is: that which surrounds an intermission.

. . . *harmony* is Now; that melody depends on what has happened while harmony is what is going to happen.

NED ROREM

Schoenberg abandoned tonality in 1908, and so began the age of "new music," with its long manifestos and tiny audiences.

Bach was music's first holy ghost—the first composer to attain a god-like posthumous fame.

ALEX ROSS

I have wept only three times in my life: the first time when my earliest opera failed, the second time when, with a boating party, a truffled turkey fell into the water, and the third time when I first heard Paganini play.

One can't judge Wagner's opera *Lohengrin* after a first hearing, and I certainly don't intend hearing it a second time.

Give me a laundry list and I'll set it to music.

Wagner has beautiful moments but awful quarter hours.

GIOACCHINO ANTONIO ROSSINI

Making music is like making love: the act is always the same, but each time it is different.

ARTUR RUBINSTEIN

Music is the nearest at hand, the most orderly, the most delicate, and the most perfect, of all bodily pleasures.

Music, when healthy, is the teacher of perfect order; and also when depraved, the teacher of perfect disorder.

JOHN RUSKIN

Paderewski is a genius who also plays the piano.

CAMILLE SAINT-SAËNS

What most people relish is hardly music; it is rather a drowsy reverie relieved by nervous thrills.

(*Music*) Something that is essentially useless, as life is.

GEORGE SANTAYANA

The sonatas of Mozart are unique: they are too easy for children, and too difficult for artists.

The notes I handle no better than many pianists. But the pauses between the notes—ah, that is where the art resides!

ARTUR SCHNABEL

Music is a shower-bath of the soul, washing away all that is impure.

ARTHUR SCHOPENHAUER

Composing gives me great pleasure. . . . There is nothing which surpasses the joy of creation, if only because through it one wins hours of self-forgetfulness, when one lives in a world of sound.

CLARA SCHUMANN

Paganini is the turning point of virtuosity.

When you play, do not trouble yourself as to who is listening. Yet always play as though a master listened to you.

People compose for many reasons: to become immortal; because the pianoforte happens to be open; because they want to become a millionaire; because of the praise of friends; because they have looked into a pair of beautiful eyes; for no reason whatsoever.

Major is the active and masculine; minor, the passive, and feminine in music.

Music owes as much to Bach as religion to its founder.

On critics:
Music induces nightingales to sing, pug-dogs to yelp.

Music resembles chess. The queen (melody) has the most power but the king (harmony) turns the scale.

Would to heaven that a race of monstrosities could arise in the world of artists, players with six fingers on each hand; then the day of virtuosodom would be at an end!

If we were all determined to play the first violin, we should never have a complete orchestra. Therefore respect every musician in his proper place.

ROBERT SCHUMANN

I must say that I think the success of those very, very modern people in painting and music is mainly due to the fact that the audience hasn't the courage to say "No."

ELIZABETH SCHWARZKOPF

I would like to hear Elliott Carter's *Fourth String Quartet*, if only to discover what a cranky prostate does to one's polyphony.

JAMES SELLARS

Music is the key to the female heart.

JOHANN G. SEUME

The nightingale, if she should sing by day,
When every goose is cackling, would be thought
No better a musician than the wren.

This music crept by me upon the waters,
Allaying both their fury, and my passion,
With its sweet air.

Though music oft hath such a charm
To make bad good, and good to provoke to harm.

Let music sound while he doth make his choice;
Then if he lose, he makes a swan-like end,
Fading in music.

Orpheus with his lute made trees,
And the mountain-tops that freeze,
Bow themselves, when he did sing.

I will play the swan
And die in music.

Give me some music; music, moody food of us
that trade in love.

Here we sit and let the sounds of music
Creep in our ears: soft stillness and the night
Became the touches of sweet harmony.

If music be the food of love, play on;
Give me excess of it, that, surfeiting,
The appetite may sicken, and so die.

The man that hath no music in himself,
Nor is not moved with concord of sweet sounds,
Is fit for treasons, stratagems and spoils.

Preposterous ass, that never read so far
To know the cause why music was ordain'd!
Was it not to refresh the mind of man,
After his studies or his usual pain?

WILLIAM SHAKESPEARE

They weren't buying music. They were doing just what they did in my day—screaming too loud to hear what they were screaming for. And stopping anyone else who wanted to hear it.

ARTIE SHAW

Hell is full of musical amateurs,
Music is the brandy of the damned.

Nothing soothes me more after a long and maddening course of pianoforte recitals than to sit and have my teeth drilled.

GEORGE BERNARD SHAW

With music sweet as love, which overflows her bower.

He is made one with Nature: there is heard
His voice in all her music, from the moan
Of thunder, to the song of night's sweet bird.

Music, when soft voices die,
Vibrates in the memory.

Sweet as stops
Of planetary music heard in trance.

PERCY BYSSHE SHELLEY

I am not legitimately married to the orchestra. I am its lover.

A statue has never yet been set up in honor of a critic.

JAN SIBELIUS

Only God can make a tree and only men can play good jazz.

GEORGE T. SIMON

My greatest teacher was not a vocal coach, not the work of other singers, but the way Tommy Dorsey breathed and phrased on the trombone.

FRANK SINATRA

I wish the government would put a tax on pianos for the incompetent.

DAME EDITH SITWELL

How could a New Yorker possibly take something called the Hollywood String Quartet seriously?

LEONARD SLATKIN

The only cheap and unpunished rapture upon earth.

SYDNEY SMITH

Music: the paradise of the ears.

SOMAIZE

One difference between poetry and lyrics is that lyrics sort of fade into the background. They fade on the page and live on the stage when set to music.

Oscar Hammerstein was a man of limited talent but infinite soul and Richard Rodgers was a man of infinite talent but limited soul.

STEPHEN SONDHEIM

Jazz will endure just as long as people hear it through their feet instead of their brains.

JOHN PHILIP SOUSA

Lady Henrietta Date says: "As one of the most beautiful young women in the older set of the younger set of society, I naturally play the bassoon. When you hunt all day and dance all night, ten quiet minutes with the bassoon prevents the weather-beaten look. . ."

MEDICAL FACTORS—Is bassoon playing considered healthy? If so, why? If not, why not? What is the yearly mortality of performers? Of listeners? Is bassoonic-homicide common?

MARK SPADE (NIGEL BALCHIN)

Melody is the sticky sweetness of music, the cloying jazz which needs background of nourishing bread before it really becomes palatable.

Jazz is not a musical form; it is a method of treatment. It is possible to take any conventional piece of music and "jazz it." The actual process is one of distorting, of rebellion against normalcy.

SIGMUND SPAETH

Dischord ofte in music makes the sweeter lay.

EDWARD SPENCER

The fine art which, more than any other, ministers to human welfare. Where there is beautiful music it is difficult for discontent to live.

HERBERT SPENCER

The habit of listening to music and of dreaming about it predisposes one to love.

STENDHAL

There are more bad musicians than there is bad music.

Everywhere in the world, music enhances a hall, with one exception: Carnegie Hall enhances the music.

ISAAC STERN

Music is feeling, then, not sound.

WALLACE STEVENS

On matters of intonation and technicalities I am more than a martinet—I am a martinetissimo.

. . . but the highest reaches of music come thrillingly close to the central core and essence of life itself.

LEOPOLD STOKOWSKI

I call the Danube blue, because it is brown and because my whimsy gives people . . . something fresh to worry over than the carryings-on of your wife with a certain Herr Glockenspieler of 19 Kapucinerstrasse, which are, I need hardly say, notorious.

JOHANN STRAUSS

In music as in love, pleasure is the waste product of creation.

I would like to admit all [Richard] Strauss's operas to whichever purgatory punishes triumphant vulgarity. Their musical substance is cheap and poor; it cannot interest a musician today.

Music is meant to be admired, not to be enjoyed.

On the Wagner festival at Bayreuth:
The place was like a crematorium, and a very old fashioned one at that. Every moment I expected to see the gentleman in black who had been entrusted with the task of singing the praises of the departed.

A good composer does not imitate; he steals.

I haven't understood a bar of music in my life, but I have felt it.

To listen is an effort, and just to hear is no merit. A duck hears also.

Too many pieces of music finish too long after the end.

Why is it that every time I hear a piece of bad music, it's by Villa-Lobos?

The trouble with music appreciation in general is that people are taught to have too much respect for music; they should be taught to love it instead.

In general, I consider that music is only able to solve musical problems; and nothing else, neither the literary nor the picturesque, can be in music of any real interest.

IGOR STRAVINSKY

Cole Porter's songs could make a shopgirl feel that she'd *been* to El Morocco or "21."

JULE STYNE

For a day and a night Love sang to us, played with us,
Folded us round from the dark and the light;
And our hearts were fulfilled with the music he made with us.

A. C. SWINBURNE

Conductors must give unmistakable and suggestive signals to the orchestra—not choreography to the audience.

I love music more than my own convenience. Actually, I love it more than myself—but it is vastly more lovable than I.

GEORGE SZELL

Is it absolutely necessary to have ideals in music? I have never given a thought of them. I have never possessed any ideals.

I played over the music of that scoundrel Brahms. What a giftless bastard.

PETER ILICH TCHAIKOVSKY

> It is the little rift within the lute,
> That by and by will make music mute,
> And ever widening, slowly silence all.
>
> The city is built
> To music, therefore never built at all,
> And therefore built forever.

Lightlier move the minutes edged with music.

Love took up the harp of Life, and smote on all the chords with
  might;
Smote the chord of Self, that, trembling, passed in music out of
  sight.

> Peace; come away: the song of woe
> Is after all an earthly song.
> Peace; come away: we do him wrong
> To sing so wildly: let us go.

ALFRED, LORD TENNYSON

On Mendelssohn:
  His face is the most beautiful face I ever saw, like what I
imagine Our Saviour's to have been.

WILLIAM MAKEPEACE THACKERAY

Schubert was a pagan with a Christian prayer in his heart.

HENRY and DANA LEE THOMAS

The God of Music dwelleth out of doors.
All seasons through his minstrelsy we meet,
Breathing by field and covert haunting-sweet.

EDITH M. THOMAS

Popular music, after all, is only familiar music.

THEODORE THOMAS

Singing is sweet, but be sure of this,
Lips only sing when they cannot kiss.

The wine of love is music,
And the feast of Love is song.

JAMES THOMSON

Music in any generation is not what the public thinks of it but what the musicians make of it.

VIRGIL THOMSON

Music is the crystallisation of sound.

Music hath caught a higher pace than any virtue I know. It is the arch-reformer; it hastens the sun to its setting; it invites him to its rising; it is the sweetest reproach, a measured satire.

HENRY DAVID THOREAU

I believe that a musician should never play anything from the point of view of pleasing the public, since the public is invariably wrong about music and particularly new music.

DAVE TOUGH, *drummer*

I don't give a damn about *The Missouri Waltz* but I can't say it out loud because it's the song of Missouri. It's as bad as *The Star Spangled Banner* so far as music is concerned.

I have read your lousy review of Margaret's concert. I've come to the conclusion that you are an "eight ulcer man on four ulcer pay." . . . Some day I hope to meet you. When that happens you'll need a new nose, a lot of beefsteak for black eyes, and perhaps a supporter below.

HARRY S TRUMAN

I always find myself stressing Mozart, which I like to call the "cereal" of the singer. The singer must digest the *leggiero* before he begins to cut into the *robusto!*

RICHARD TUCKER

Listening to Wagner's music is like having a toothache in the pit of the stomach.

MARK TWAIN

Music is a language directed to the passions; but the rudest passions put on a new nature and become pleasing in harmony.

JAMES USHER

On jazz:
Music invented by demons for the torture of imbeciles.

HENRY VAN DYKE

My best work is a home for destitute musicians that I have endowed in Milan.

GIUSEPPE VERDI

The Most High has a decided taste for vocal music, provided it be lugubrious and gloomy enough.

Anything that is too stupid to be spoken is sung.

VOLTAIRE

On Richard Strauss:
   When it comes to Richard, I prefer Wagner. And when it comes to Strauss, I prefer Johann.

HANS VON BULOW, *pianist*

I dreamt all this: never could my poor head have invented such a thing purposely.

Isolation and complete loneliness are my only consolation, and my salvation.

Works of art cannot be created at present, they can only be prepared for by means of revolutionary activity, by destroying and crushing everything that is worth destroying and crushing.

I have an enormous desire to commit acts of artistic terrorism.

Women are the music of life.

RICHARD WAGNER

All music is singing. The ideal is to make the orchestra play like singers.

BRUNO WALTER

I can't sing. As a singist I am not a success. I am saddest
when I sing. So are those who hear me. They are sadder even
than I am.

ARTEMUS WARD (CHARLES FARRAR BROWNE)

Music is the true universal speech of mankind.

WEBER

Donny Osmond has van Gogh's ear for music.

ORSON WELLES

Music comes before religion, as emotion comes before
thought, and sound before sense. What is the first thing you
hear when you go into a church? The organ playing.

ALFRED NORTH WHITEHEAD

Those were the years! In 1925, I grossed $680,000—before
taxes—thank the Lord. Around 1922 our band played for a
party for Clarence Mackay . . . and I got a $10,000 tip myself—
not unusual in those days.

Jazz came to America three hundred years ago in chains.

PAUL WHITEMAN

The strongest and sweetest songs yet remain to be sung.

I see America go singing to her destiny.

All music is what awakes from you when you are reminded by
    the instruments,
It is not the violins and the cornets, it is not the oboe nor the
    beating drums, nor the score of the baritone singer singing
    his sweet romanza, nor that of the men's chorus, nor that
    of the women's chorus.
It is nearer and farther than they.

WALT WHITMAN

Good music is wine turned to sound.

ELLA WHEELER WILCOX

After playing Chopin, I feel as if I had been weeping over
sins that I had never committed.

Life has been your art. You have set yourself to music. Your
days are your sonnets.

Of course, the music is a great difficulty. You see, if one plays
good music, people don't listen, and if one plays bad music
people don't talk.

> Her ivory hands on the ivory keys
>   Strayed in a fitful fantasy,
> Like the silver gleam when the poplar trees
>   Rustle their pale leaves listlessly.

If one hears bad music it is one's duty to drown it by one's
conversation.

I like Wagner's music better than any other music. It is so
loud that one can talk the whole time without people hearing
what one says. That is a great advantage.

Over the piano was printed a notice:
"Please do not shoot the pianist. He is doing his best."

OSCAR WILDE

A man can find out more about himself and his power of inner thinking through his reaction to music than all the Freuds or Jungs that have ever lived could tell him.

ALBERT S. WILLIAMS

A supreme composer can only come out of a musical nation.

VAUGHN WILLIAMS

The success of today's rock songs proves one thing—rhyme doesn't pay.

EARL WILSON

The man who disparages music as a luxury and non-essential is doing the nation an injury. Music now, more than ever before, is a national need. There is no better way to express patriotism than through music.

WOODROW WILSON

You could tell it was classical music, because the banjo-players were leaning back and chewing gum; and in New York restaurants only death or a classical speciality can stop banjoists.

Musical comedy is the Irish stew of drama. Anything may be put into it, with the certainty that it will improve the general effect.

An accordian, or stomach Steinway.

The plaintive sound of saxophones moaning softly like a man who has just missed a short putt.

P. G. WODEHOUSE

Books! 'tis a dull and endless strife:
   Come, hear the woodland linnet,
How sweet his music! on my life,
   There's more of wisdom in it.

And hark! how blithe the throstle sings!
   He, too, is no mean preacher:
Come forth into the light of things,
   Let nature be your teacher.

WILLIAM WORDSWORTH

A musician who would give me pleasure should not repeat a line or put more than one note to a syllable.

WILLIAM BUTLER YEATS

A musical talent is like having six fingers on one hand. You're born with it, you're different because of it, you can't do a thing about it except put it to use.

Bop is just Stravinsky played on an empty stomach.

FLORIAN ZABACH, *violinist*

There are more love songs than anything else. If songs could make you do something we'd all love one another.

FRANK ZAPPA

NONFICTION

OF THE LIFE OF FREDERICK DOUGLASS, Frederick Douglass. 96pp. 28499-9

LIANCE AND OTHER ESSAYS, Ralph Waldo Emerson. 128pp. 0-486-27790-9

LIFE OF OLAUDAH EQUIANO, OR GUSTAVUS VASSA, THE AFRICAN, Olaudah Equiano. 92pp. 0-486-40661-X

HE AUTOBIOGRAPHY OF BENJAMIN FRANKLIN, Benjamin Franklin. 144pp. 0-486-29073-5

TOTEM AND TABOO, Sigmund Freud. 176pp. (Not available in Europe or United Kingdom.) 0-486-40434-X

LOVE: A Book of Quotations, Herb Galewitz (ed.). 64pp. 0-486-40004-2

PRAGMATISM, William James. 128pp. 0-486-28270-8

THE STORY OF MY LIFE, Helen Keller. 80pp. 0-486-29249-5

TAO TE CHING, Lao Tze. 112pp. 0-486-29792-6

GREAT SPEECHES, Abraham Lincoln. 112pp. 0-486-26872-1

THE PRINCE, Niccolò Machiavelli. 80pp. 0-486-27274-5

THE SUBJECTION OF WOMEN, John Stuart Mill. 112pp. 0-486-29601-6

SELECTED ESSAYS, Michel de Montaigne. 96pp. 0-486-29109-X

UTOPIA, Sir Thomas More. 96pp. 0-486-29583-4

BEYOND GOOD AND EVIL: Prelude to a Philosophy of the Future, Friedrich Nietzsche. 176pp. 0-486-29868-X

THE BIRTH OF TRAGEDY, Friedrich Nietzsche. 96pp. 0-486-28515-4

COMMON SENSE, Thomas Paine. 64pp. 0-486-29602-4

SYMPOSIUM AND PHAEDRUS, Plato. 96pp. 0-486-27798-4

THE TRIAL AND DEATH OF SOCRATES: Four Dialogues, Plato. 128pp. 0-486-27066-1

A MODEST PROPOSAL AND OTHER SATIRICAL WORKS, Jonathan Swift. 64pp. 0-486-28759-9

CIVIL DISOBEDIENCE AND OTHER ESSAYS, Henry David Thoreau. 96pp. 0-486-27563-9

WALDEN; OR, LIFE IN THE WOODS, Henry David Thoreau. 224pp. 0-486-28495-6

NARRATIVE OF SOJOURNER TRUTH, Sojourner Truth. 80pp. 0-486-29899-X

THE THEORY OF THE LEISURE CLASS, Thorstein Veblen. 256pp. 0-486-28062-4

DE PROFUNDIS, Oscar Wilde. 64pp. 0-486-29308-4

OSCAR WILDE'S WIT AND WISDOM: A Book of Quotations, Oscar Wilde. 64pp. 0-486-40146-4

UP FROM SLAVERY, Booker T. Washington. 160pp. 0-486-28738-6

A VINDICATION OF THE RIGHTS OF WOMAN, Mary Wollstonecraft. 224pp. 0-486-29036-0

PLAYS

PROMETHEUS BOUND, Aeschylus. 64pp. 0-486-28762-9

THE ORESTEIA TRILOGY: Agamemnon, The Libation-Bearers and The Furies, Aeschylus. 160pp. 0-486-29242-8

LYSISTRATA, Aristophanes. 64pp. 0-486-28225-2

WHAT EVERY WOMAN KNOWS, James Barrie. 80pp. (Not available in Europe or United Kingdom.) 0-486-29578-8

THE CHERRY ORCHARD, Anton Chekhov. 64pp. 0-486-26682-6

THE SEA GULL, Anton Chekhov. 64pp. 0-486-40656-3

THE THREE SISTERS, Anton Chekhov. 64pp. 0-486-27544-2

UNCLE VANYA, Anton Chekhov. 64pp. 0-486-40159-6

THE WAY OF THE WORLD, William Congreve. 80pp. 0-486-27787-9

BACCHAE, Euripides. 64pp. 0-486-29580-X

MEDEA, Euripides. 64pp. 0-486-27548-5

PLAYS

ELECTRA, Sophocles. 64pp. 0-486-28482-4

MISS JULIE, August Strindberg. 64pp. 0-486-27281-8

THE PLAYBOY OF THE WESTERN WORLD AND RIDERS TO THE SEA, 0-486-27562-0

THE DUCHESS OF MALFI, John Webster. 96pp. 0-486-40660-1

THE IMPORTANCE OF BEING EARNEST, Oscar Wilde. 64pp. 0-486-26478-5

LADY WINDERMERE'S FAN, Oscar Wilde. 64pp. 0-486-40078-6

BOXED SETS

FAVORITE JANE AUSTEN NOVELS: *Pride and Prejudice, Sense and Sensibility* and *Persuasion* (Complete and Unabridged), Jane Austen. 800pp. 0-486-29748-9

BEST WORKS OF MARK TWAIN: Four Books, Dover. 624pp. 0-486-40226-6

EIGHT GREAT GREEK TRAGEDIES: Six Books, Dover. 480pp. 0-486-40203-7

FIVE GREAT ENGLISH ROMANTIC POETS, Dover. 496pp. 0-486-27893-X

GREAT AFRICAN-AMERICAN WRITERS: Seven Books, Dover. 704pp. 0-486-29995-3

GREAT WOMEN POETS: 4 Complete Books, Dover. 256pp. (Available in U.S. only.) 0-486-28388-7

MASTERPIECES OF RUSSIAN LITERATURE: Seven Books, Dover. 880pp. 0-486-40665-2

SIX GREAT AMERICAN POETS: Poems by Poe, Dickinson, Whitman, Longfellow, Frost, and Millay, Dover. 512pp. (Available in U.S. only.) 0-486-27425-X

FAVORITE NOVELS AND STORIES: Four Complete Books, Jack London. 568pp. 0-486-42216-X

FIVE GREAT SCIENCE FICTION NOVELS, H. G. Wells. 640pp. 0-486-43978-X

FIVE GREAT PLAYS OF SHAKESPEARE, Dover. 496pp. 0-486-27892-1

TWELVE PLAYS BY SHAKESPEARE, William Shakespeare. 1,173pp. 0-486-44336-1